MAN CAVE
DUMB JOKES

—— · ——

by

Jack Kreismer

RED-LETTER PRESS, INC.
Saddle River, New Jersey

Red-Letter Press, Inc.
P.O. Box 393
Saddle River, NJ 07458

www.Red-LetterPress.com

ACKNOWLEDGMENTS

BOOK DESIGN & TYPOGRAPHY:
Jeff Kreismer

·

COVER & INTERIOR ART:
Andrew Towl

·

RESEARCH & DEVELOPMENT:
Kobus Reyneke

·

CONTRIBUTORS:
Tim McVeigh
Chuckie Ward

MAN CAVE
DUMB JOKES

SERIOUSLY DUMB…

Teacher: Where is the English Channel?

Student: I don't know anymore. We switched cable companies last month.

• • •

A guy walks into a lumberyard and asks for some two-by-fours. The clerk asks, "How long do you need them?"

The guy answers, "A long time. We're gonna build a house."

• • •

A teen is arrested and put in the police station jail for smoking pot. The officer on duty allows the delinquent to make one call and then brings him to his cell. Forty-five minutes later, a guy shows up at the jail. "You must be the boy's father," says the cop.

"No," says the man. "I'm here with the pizza delivery."

This fellow walks by an optometrist's shop. Displayed in the storefront window is a gigantic pair of sunglasses accompanied by a sign, "Nudie Sunglasses!" The chap is intrigued, goes inside and asks the optometrist about them. The optometrist says, "Try them on and see for yourself."

The guy tries on the giant sunglasses, looks at the optometrist and can't believe what he sees. The optometrist appears totally naked! "Does this mean that when I put on these sunglasses everyone becomes nude?"

"That's right."

Well, the guy just has to have them, so he buys a pair and heads home. When he gets there, he opens the door, puts on his new nudie sunglasses and walks into the living room. There he sees his wife sitting on the couch with his neighbor, both appearing to be stark naked.

"You're not going to believe this, Dear," says the guy, "but I just bought these super duper sunglasses."

He takes them off to show her and notices the wife and neighbor are still nude. "Geez," he complains, "I've only had these sunglasses half an hour and they're broken already!"

Herb is telling Wally about the brand new thermos he brought along for their camping trip. "It's great," he said. "The guy at the store where I bought it told me it keeps hot things hot and cold things cold."

"Sweet," said Wally. "What do you have in it?"

"Three coffees and an ice cream sandwich."

• • •

A fellow is driving down a heavily flooded road after a torrential rainstorm when, all of the sudden, he sees a guy's head sticking out of a huge puddle. He stops and asks the guy if he needs a ride. The guy answers, "Nah, that's ok. I'm on my bike."

• • •

The king is moose hunting in the woods with one of his henchmen. Suddenly, they spot another fellow a distance away. The king raises his rifle and aims it at him. The fellow yells out, "I am not a moose!!!"

The king fires at the man and kills him. "Your highness!" his startled henchman exclaims. "He said he wasn't a moose!"

The king says, "Oh— I thought he said, 'I am a moose.'"

The first day on the new job, a budding lumberjack managed to cut down only three trees. While the boss wasn't too concerned, as time went on, no progress was made.

Finally, the boss called the lumberjack into his office for an interview to find out what the trouble was. "I don't understand it boss, I work as hard as I can- I don't even take breaks or lunch."

"Well son," his boss said understandingly, "maybe it's your equipment- could be your chain saw."

"No I checked that- it's sharp enough."

Checking to see if the saw ran properly, the boss pulled the cord and it cranked right up. Startled, the employee jumped a foot off his seat, looked around and shouted, "What's that noise?"

CAVE DWELLINGS

I'll be long gone before some smart person ever figures out what happened inside this Oval Office.

-President George W. Bush

Chester: A man knocked on my door today and asked for a small donation for the local swimming pool.

Lester: What did you give him?

Chester: A glass of water.

• • •

Harry: I'm thinking of getting a dog- and I think I want a Labrador.

Larry: That might not be such a good idea. Have you seen how many of their owners go blind?

• • •

A woman is grocery shopping in the meat department and says to the butcher, "I'll take two pork chops- and please make them lean."

"Sure," says the butcher. "Which way?"

• • •

Two simple-minded fellows are walking down the street when one of them sees a broken mirror on the ground. He picks it up, looks at it and says, "This guy looks very familiar, but I can't quite place him."

The second fellow grabs the mirror from him, looks at it and says, "It's me, you dummy!"

Willy was getting ready for his first parachute jump. The last thing his instructor said to him was, "Remember Willy, once you're out, count to five and pull this cord for the primary chute. If that fails, pull this cord for the back-up chute. Keep your legs loose when you land and while you roll up your chute, a truck will head out to get you."

With that, the instructor pushed Willy out of the plane. Willy counted to five and then pulled the cord for his main chute. It didn't deploy so he pulled the cord for his back-up chute. It didn't deploy, either.

As Willy was plummeting towards the earth, he thought, "Great! The way my luck's been going today, the truck's probably not gonna show up either."

CAVE DWELLINGS

Good pitching will always stop good hitting, and vice-versa.

-Casey Stengel, Hall of Fame baseball manager

Two guys are working in a gymnastics equipment factory. One says to the other, "I'm gonna make the boss give me a day off."

The other guy says, "How are you going to do that?"

"Watch," the first guy says. With that, he drapes his feet around a nearly ceiling-high horizontal bar and hangs from it.

His boss comes in the room, sees him and says, "What are you doing?"

He says, "I'm a light bulb."

With a perplexed look, the boss says, "You've been working too hard. I think it's driving you crazy. You better go home and get some rest."

The guy starts to leave, but when the second guy starts to follow him, the boss says, "Where do you think you're going?"

He replies, "I'm going home, too. I can't see in the dark."

• • •

Did you hear about the invisible man and invisible woman's kids?

They're not much to look at.

One snowy morning a husband and wife wake up and hear the latest forecast on the radio. "Five to six inches more of the white stuff is expected. Alternate side of the street parking is in effect. You can only park on the even numbered side of the street today, folks."

With that, the wife gets dressed, goes out and moves her car to the other side of the street.

A week later she hears a similar forecast. "Three to six inches expected this morning. Parking on only the odd numbered side of the street today."

The wife goes out and moves the car again.

A few days later comes this radio announcement: "We're going to be hit with a big snowstorm today. As far as parking goes..."

All of the sudden, the power is lost! The worried wife turns to her husband and says, "Now I don't know where to park my car. What should I do?"

The husband answers, "I'd say you should just leave it in the garage."

CHICKEN JOKES

Inquiring minds want to know...Who was the first person to say, "See that chicken right there? I'm gonna eat the next thing that comes outta its butt."

• • •

A religious cowboy lost his pocket Bible while he was fixing fences out on the range. Lo and behold, a couple of weeks later, a chicken sauntered up to him carrying the mini-book in its mouth. The cowboy took the Bible and looked heavenward, exclaiming, "It's a miracle!"

"Not exactly," said the chicken. "Your name is written inside the cover."

CAVE DWELLINGS

Beauty fades...
dumb is forever.

-Judge Judy

A chicken crosses the road to go to the library. It walks inside and says to the librarian, "Book."

The librarian says, "You want a book?"

"Book."

"Any old book?"

"Book."

The librarian gives the chicken a novel and off it goes. A couple of hours later the chicken comes back and says, "Book-book."

The librarian says, "Now you're telling me that you want two books?"

"Book-book."

She gives the chicken two more novels. The chicken leaves again only to come back one more time saying, "Book-book-book."

"Three books?"

"Book-book-book."

The librarian gives the chicken three more novels. At this point, the librarian's curiosity is piqued so she decides to follow the chicken to see what's going on.

She trails the chicken as it leaves the library, goes down the road, out of town, into the woods and down to a swamp where there is a bullfrog. The chicken hands the books to him.

The bullfrog looks at the novels and says, "Reddit... Reddit...Reddit."

• • •

Why did Beethoven get rid of his chicken?

It kept saying, "Bach, Bach, Bach, Bach, Bach..."

• • •

What did the chick say when it saw an orange in the nest?

"Look at the orange mama laid."

CAVE DWELLINGS

I should have read it before it came out.

-Charles Barkley, on being misquoted in his autobiography

Colonel Sanders was driving along a rural Kentucky road one day when he saw a three-legged chicken running down the dusty byway. His professional curiosity was aroused enough to drive alongside it for a while, and clock it at 30 mph. "Pretty fast chicken," he thought. "I wonder just how fast it can run."

He sped up and the chicken kept pace. They were now moving along the road at 45 mph. Sanders sped up again but to his surprise, the chicken was still running ahead of him at 60 mph. Suddenly, the chicken turned off the road and zoomed down a long driveway leading to a farmhouse. Sanders followed the chicken and saw a man in the yard with dozens of three-legged chickens. Colonel Sanders couldn't believe his eyes.

He called out to the farmer, "How did you get all these three-legged chickens?"

The farmer replied, "I breed 'em. Ya see, we're a family of three and we all like chicken legs. We were always one short, so I started breeding this three-legged variety so we could each have our favorite piece."

"That's amazing!" said Colonel Sanders. "How do they taste?"

"Don't rightly know," the farmer drawled. "I ain't caught one yet!"

What religious man are chickens afraid of?

The friar.

• • •

Patient: Doc, my wife thinks I'm crazy because I like chicken wings.

Psychiatrist: That's not crazy. I like chicken wings, too.

Patient: Great! You gotta come over and see my collection! I've got thousands of 'em!

• • •

What do you call a chicken that crosses the road?

Poultry in motion.

CAVE DWELLINGS

I never apologize. I'm sorry, but that's just the way I am.

-Homer Simpson

Why did the chicken cross the road?

Because the light turned green.

Why did the chicken cross the road?

It was trying out a new pair of roller skates.

Why did the chicken cross the road?

Well, he was feeling sprite, it was a beautiful day, there was no traffic in sight, visibility was good, and all the other chickens happened to be doing it.

Why did the chicken cross the road?

To get to the movie theater to watch a chick flick.

Why did the chicken cross the road?

To help the little old lady across the street.

Why did the chicken cross the road?

To prove to the possum it could actually be done.

Why did the chicken cross the road?

To get away from all those stupid chicken jokes.

Why didn't the chicken cross the road?
Because there was a KFC on the other side.

Why didn't the chicken cross the road?
Because he was chicken.

Why did the turkey cross the road?
To prove he wasn't chicken.

• • •

Q: Why did the chicken cross the Internet?
A: To get to the other site.

Q: Why did the chicken cross the playground?
A: To get to the other slide.

Q: Why did the chewing gum cross the road?
A: Because it was stuck to the chicken!

Q: Why did the dinosaur cross the road?
A: Chickens hadn't been invented yet.

Why did Donald Trump cross the road?

He heard there was a comb-over on the other side.

Why did the pope cross the road?

He crosses everything.

Why did the turtle cross the road?

To get to the shell station.

Why did the spider cross the road?

To get to his web site!

• • •

A duck was about to cross the road and the chicken said, "Don't do it, Dude. You'll never hear the end of it."

CAVE DWELLINGS

A zebra does not change its spots.

-Al Gore

DUMB DOCTOR JOKES

A guy goes to a psychiatrist and says, "My wife thinks I'm crazy because I like plaid socks."

"That's not so strange," replies the doctor. "As a matter of fact, I kind of like them, too."

"Really?" exclaimed the patient, excited to find a sympathetic ear. "Do you like yours with chocolate fudge or Hollandaise sauce?"

• • •

Patient: Doc, you gotta help me. My wife thinks she's an elevator.

Psychiatrist: Bring her in to see me.

Patient: I can't. She doesn't stop on this floor!

A guy goes to a psychiatrist and says, "Doc, you gotta help me."

The shrink says, "What's your problem?"

He says, "Oh, it's not me. It's my wife. She thinks she's a lawn mower."

"How long has this been going on?" asks the doctor.

"Oh, for about a year and a half."

The doctor says, "Why didn't you bring her in here sooner?"

"I couldn't, Doc. The last guy who borrowed her didn't return her for six months."

CAVE DWELLINGS

I think there's a difference between ditzy and dumb. Dumb is just not knowing. Ditzy is having the courage to ask!

-Jessica Simpson

Patient: Doctor, I keep seeing double!

Doctor: Please, have a seat on the couch.

Patient: Which one?

• • •

Patient: Doc, I think I'm a goat.

Doctor: How long have you had this feeling?

Patient: Ever since I was a kid.

• • •

Patient: Doc, my head hurts.

Doctor: I think I see the problem. You've got a piece of lettuce hanging out of your ear.

Patient: That's just the tip of the iceberg.

• • •

Patient: Doctor, my hands won't stop shaking!

Doctor: Do you drink a lot?

Patient: No, I spill most of it.

• • •

Patient: I bought a pair of shoes from a drug dealer.

Doctor: So?

Patient: I don't know what he laced them with, but I've been tripping all day.

Mom: Doc, my little boy runs around all day going "cluck, cluck, cluck" like a chicken.

Doctor: Can't you break him of the habit?

Mom: I'm afraid to.

Doctor: Why?

Mom: We need the eggs.

• • •

Patient: Doc, I know you say I have a split personality, but is it okay for me to get married?

Doctor: Sure ... Who are you planning to marry?

Patient: The Jones twins.

• • •

Patient: Doc, I need help. I keep thinking that I'm a horse.

Doctor: I think I can cure you, but it's going to take some time and it's going to be extremely expensive.

Patient: Money's not a problem, Doc. I just won the Kentucky Derby.

• • •

Patient: Doctor, I just ate an orange ball, a red ball and a blue ball. I feel horrible!

Doctor: No wonder. You're not eating enough greens!

Patient: Doc, help me. I've got a strawberry growing out of my head.

Doctor: I'll give you some cream to put on it.

• • •

Doctor: I don't know how to tell you this, but you only have three minutes to live.

Patient: Isn't there anything you can do for me?

Doctor: Would you like me to boil you an egg?

• • •

Patient: Every time I drink a cup of coffee, I get a stabbing pain in my left eye. What should I do, Doc?

Doctor: Take the spoon out of your cup.

CAVE DWELLINGS

The world is more like it is now than it ever has been before.

-President Dwight Eisenhower

Patient: Doctor, Doctor, I need help.

Dentist: What's the problem?

Patient: I think I'm a moth.

Dentist: You don't need a dentist. You need a psychiatrist.

Patient: Yes, I know.

Dentist: So why did you come in here?

Patient: The light was on.

• • •

Patient: What- I can't be cured!? That's horrible! How much time do I have, Doc?

Doctor: Ten...

Patient: Ten years? Ten months? What?!?!

Doctor: Nine, eight...

CAVE DWELLINGS

Sometimes they write what I say and not what I mean.

-Pedro Guerrero, former baseball player, on the media

COP JOKES

One evening, a policeman was staking out a tavern for possible driving-under-the-influence violations. When the bar closed, he saw a fellow come staggering out, fumble with his keys and get into his car. Finally, he started the engine and took off, only to find the cop waiting for him.

The officer approached the driver and gave the guy a breathalyzer test. The results showed a reading of zero. The cop demanded to know how that could be.

The guy responded, "Tonight, I'm the designated decoy."

• • •

A guy staggers out of a bar and realizes he's in no shape to drive. He leaves his car there and starts to walk home. As he's stumbling along, a cop stops him and says, "What's up buddy?"

"I'm goin' to a lecture," slurs the guy.

"At two in the morning? Just who is giving a lecture at this hour?" the cop suspiciously asks.

"My wife."

Riley was speeding down the road at seventy miles per hour. He was pulled over by a cop who said, "Do you know the speed limit is fifty five miles per hour?"

"Yes, officer," replied Riley, looking as innocent as possible, "but I wasn't going to be out that long."

• • •

A cop wrote out a speeding ticket. The recipient angrily began waving it in the air and said, "What am I supposed to do with this?"

"Keep it," said the cop. "When you collect three more, you get a bicycle."

• • •

A priest is driving home from a St. Patrick's Day party and absentmindedly leaves an empty wine bottle on the floor of the passenger side of the car. He gets pulled over by a cop, who smells alcohol on the priest's breath and notices the wine bottle on the floor. The cop says, "Father, have you been drinking?"

"No, just water," answers the priest.

The cop says, "Then how come I smell wine?"

The priest excitedly says, "My God! He's done it again!!"

In the backwoods of Georgia, a county sheriff observed a truck driver pull off the side of the road, get out of his vehicle and pound on the sides of his trailer. Thinking it a bit suspicious, the sheriff followed at a discreet distance.

A few minutes later, the truck driver pulled off the side of the road again, got out and pounded the sides of his trailer. The third time the truck driver pulled off, the sheriff switched on his lights and sounded the siren. Ambling up to the truck driver, who was again pounding on the side of his trailer, the sheriff drawled, "Now just what do you think you're doing, Boy?"

"Simple, officer," said the truck driver. "I got fifteen tons of canaries in here and the load limit is ten tons so I got to keep some of them flying around."

CAVE DWELLINGS

I made a misstatement and I stand by all my misstatements.

-Dan Quayle,
U.S. Vice-President

What *do* you call twin police officers?

Copies

• • •

Herb: I got stopped by a cop the other day.

Ralph: Oh, yeah? What happened?

Herb: He made me get out of the car, walk a straight line, recite the alphabet and then he shined a flashlight in my face and said, "Your eyes look bloodshot. You been drinkin'?"

Ralph: What did you say?

Herb: I said, "Why, no, officer. But your eyes look glazed. Have you been eating donuts?"

CAVE DWELLINGS

Life is hard; it's harder if you're stupid.

-John Wayne

A man and his wife were out for a drive when a cop pulled them over. As the officer approached the car, the man rolled down his window.

The cop said, "Excuse me, sir. Were you aware that you were driving well over the speed limit?"

The driver responded, "Why, no officer, I wasn't aware of that."

With that, his wife exclaimed, "Who are you kidding? You were going at least 20 miles over the limit!"

The cop then asked, "And I noticed you weren't wearing a seat belt. How come?"

He answered, "Well, officer, when I saw you approach the car I figured I'd probably have to get out so I took it off."

His wife then said, "What are you talking about? You never wear a seat belt."

At that point, the cop leaned in and said to the wife, "Does your husband always lie like this?"

"Oh, not always officer," she replied, "only when he's had too much to drink."

THREE DUMB KNOCK KNOCKS

Knock knock.

Who's there?

Interrupting cow.

Interrupti...

MOOOOOOOOOOOOOOOOOOOOOOOOOOOOOOOO!

• • •

Knock Knock.

Who's there?

Control freak... Now you say, "Control freak who?"

• • •

Knock Knock.

Who's there?

To.

To who?

No, it's to whom.

DUMB LAWYER JOKES

A guy walks into a lawyer's office and asks, "What are your rates?"

"Two hundred dollars for three questions," answers the lawyer.

"That's a pretty hefty charge, isn't it?" retorts the man.

"Maybe," the lawyer responds. "What's your final question?"

• • •

A lawyer, meeting with his client in prison, says, "I've got some good news and bad news."

The client says, "Gimme the bad news first."

"Your DNA matches the blood found on the victim as well as the murder weapon."

"What could the good news possibly be?" asks the client.

"Your cholesterol is down to 120."

Q: What's the difference between a trampoline and a lawyer?

A: You take your shoes off to jump on a trampoline.

Q: What's the difference between a lawyer and a liar?

A: The pronunciation.

Q: What's the difference between an onion and a lawyer?

A: When you cut the onion, you cry.

Q: What's black and brown and looks good on a lawyer?

A: A Doberman.

Q: What do you get when you cross a lawyer with a snake?

A: Incest.

Q: What would you get if you crossed a cockroach with a lawyer?

A: Nothing. Even cockroaches have some standards.

An extremely inebriated fellow walks into a bar, climbs on top of a barstool and shouts, "All lawyers are idiots!"

A guy down at the end of the bar says, "I resent that remark."

The drunk yells back, "Why, are you a lawyer?"

"No, I'm an idiot."

• • •

Terrorists raided the annual attorneys' convention in New York and held all the lawyers hostage. They threatened that until their demands were met, they'd release a lawyer every hour.

CAVE DWELLINGS

I'm not going for the Sixteenth Chapel.

-Justin Bieber, when told that too many tattoos would make him look like Michelangelo's art in the Sistine Chapel

WIFE AND MOTHER IN LAW JOKES

After a knock-down, drag-out fight, a wife complained to her husband, "You know, I was a fool when I married you!"

He replied, "Yeah, sweetheart, but I was in love and didn't notice it."

. . .

An elderly retired couple were discussing their future. "What will you do if I should die before you?" the husband asked.

The wife thought for a moment and replied, "Oh, I guess I'd look for a situation where I could share a place with two or three single or widowed women. I think I'd prefer them to be younger than I am since I'm still very active... What would you do if I die first?"

He replied, "I guess I'd do the same thing."

Two buddies met at a bar and one asked the other how things were going.

"Not so hot- had an argument with the wife," was his answer.

"What happened?" asked his friend sympathetically.

"We had money troubles so she told me I couldn't buy beer by the case anymore. Then I caught her paying $50 a bottle for nail polish off a TV shopping channel."

"That's not right."

"Yeah, and then she went to a beauty parlor and had a $250 makeover."

"So what'd you do?"

"I confronted her and demanded to know why she was wasting all that money."

"What did she say?"

"She said that she had to. She needed all that stuff so that she could look prettier for me."

"What'd you say?"

"I said, 'Are you crazy? That's what the beer was for in the first place.'"

Three guys are on their lunch break, talking about their wives. Two of them are bragging about how they're the "man of the house" while the third remains silent.

After a while, one of the guys says to the third fellow, "You've been pretty quiet, pal. What's the matter- does your wife boss you around?"

The third guy says, "Let me tell you guys something. Just the other night, my wife came to me crawling on her hands and knees."

The first two guys look at him astonishingly and one says, "What was the reason for that?"

"She said, 'Get out from under that bed and fight like a man you little weasel.'"

CAVE DWELLINGS

If I die before my cat, I want a little of my ashes put in his food so I can live inside him.

-Drew Barrymore

A husband and wife were vacationing on a cross country trip. As they passed through a rural area, they began to quibble about the pronunciation of a small town. Finally, they decided to stop at a fast food place to ask one of the local folk how to pronounce it.

They walked into the restaurant, placed an order with the waitress, and the wife asked, "Could you please tell us where we are and, if you don't mind, say it real slow?"

The waitress said, "Listen very closely... M-c-D-O-N-A-L-D-S."

• • •

A man was riding a bicycle built for two all alone when he was pulled over by the police. "What's the problem, Officer?" he asked.

"Perhaps you hadn't noticed, but your wife fell off a half-mile back," the officer replied.

"Oh, thank God," the bicyclist said as he wiped his brow. "I was afraid that I had gone deaf!"

Harvey had been in and out of a coma for several months. His wife stayed by his side every moment. One evening he came to, and called her over to his bed.

She sat by him and tears welled up in her eyes as he said, "My darling, you were with me all along, always at my side. When I got fired, you were there. When I got charged with tax evasion, you were there. When my business went bankrupt, you were there. And now, my health is failing and you are here. You know what?"

"What my dear? Tell me what," she implored, her voice cracking with emotion.

Harvey drew his last gasp of air and replied, "I'm beginning to think you're bad luck."

CAVE DWELLINGS

I think that gay marriage is something that should be between a man and a woman.

-Arnold Schwarzenegger

A couple having a candlelit dinner to celebrate their silver wedding anniversary were surprised by the sudden appearance of the Fairy Godmother. "You have had such a wonderful relationship all these years that I will reward you with anything you ask," she announced.

The woman said, "I always wanted to take a romantic around-the-world cruise with my husband."

The Fairy Godmother waved her wand and -poof! - two tickets appeared in the woman's hand. Then it was the husband's turn.

"I hate to say this, but you only get a wish like this once and I always wanted to be married to a woman about 25 years younger than me."

His wife was crushed, totally crestfallen. "Sorry, Dear, but that's what I want," he said.

"But Honey," the wife pleaded, "don't leave me."

"Forget it," he snorted, "I want a wife 25 years younger than me and that's that." He then signaled the Fairy Godmother to make it so.

The Fairy Godmother nodded, waved her wand and- poof- the man got his wish. He became 95 years old.

A husband is on his way out to the store when the wife says, "Please pick up a carton of milk and if they have eggs, get me a dozen."

The husband returns home with 12 cartons of milk.

"Why on earth would you get me 12 cartons of milk?" asks the wife.

"They had eggs."

• • •

Charlie took his wife and mother-in-law to the Holy Land. While they were visiting Jerusalem, his mother-in-law suddenly dropped dead. He went to the American Consulate to make arrangements.

"Shipping a body back to the States is a very expensive business," the consul warned. "It can cost upwards of ten thousand dollars. But if you bury the body here it's only about three hundred."

"Hmm," Charlie rubbed his chin and thought for a moment, "No, I'm having her shipped home no matter how much it costs. Someone rose from the dead here once before and I'm just not willing to take that chance."

Maxy Segal, serving 10 years in the pen, got a letter from his wife: "Dear Maxy, I wanted to grow some lettuce but since you're the one with the green thumb, I wondered when would be the best time to plant it in the garden."

Knowing that the guards read all the prisoners' mail, he replied: "My Dear Wife, whatever you do, don't dig up the garden. I buried the loot from the heist there!"

About a week later, Maxy received another letter from his better half: "Dear Maxy, I don't know what happened. A few days ago, fifty men with shovels showed up and dug up the entire garden."

Maxy sent his reply immediately: "My Dear Wife, it is now time to plant."

CAVE DWELLINGS

I was asked to come to Chicago because Chicago is one of our 52 states.

-Raquel Welch

A minister and his very conservative wife had a great marriage except for his long business trips and lifelong obsession with golf. One day while he was away, she was cleaning and found a box of mementos in the back of the bedroom closet. In it, she found three golf balls and $800.

That night when he called, she asked him the meaning of the three golf balls. He said, "Well dear, I've been keeping that box for twenty years. I'm ashamed to admit it but so great is my passion for the game of golf that I occasionally swear on the course. Every time I use unsavory language, I penalize myself one golf ball."

Shocked that her husband, a man of the cloth, would ever use four-letter words, the wife was at first taken aback but then thought, "Well, three balls means that he's only cursed three times in twenty years. I suppose that isn't so bad."

"All right dear," she said, "I forgive you for your lapses, but tell me, what's the $800 for?"

"Oh that," answered the minister. "I found a guy who buys golf balls at two bucks a dozen."

If a man says something in the middle of the forest and there is no woman around to hear him...is he still wrong?

• • •

Wife: How would you describe me?

Hubby: You are ABCDEFGHIJK.

Wife: What's that supposed to mean?

Hubby: Adorable, beautiful, cute, delightful, elegant, first-class, gorgeous, and hot.

Wife: Aw, thank you... but what about IJK?

Hubby: I'm just kidding!

• • •

Mabel tells Gertrude of her husband's untimely death. "Poor old Harold was out in the vegetable patch to get me some greens, when all of the sudden he dropped dead of a heart attack."

"Oh, my goodness. What a tragedy! What ever did you do?" asks Gertrude.

"I had to defrost some string beans."

Ralph forgot his wedding anniversary and his wife was more than a bit agitated. "Tomorrow morning, I expect to find a gift in the driveway that goes from 0 to 200 in five seconds. And it better be there or else!" she yelled.

The next morning Ralph woke up early to do his thing. When his wife got up, she looked out the window and, sure enough, there was a gift-wrapped box, smack in the middle of the driveway.

The wife put on her robe and slippers, ran outside and opened up the gift- a bathroom scale.

• • •

Why did the Amish couple divorce?

Because he was driving her buggy.

CAVE DWELLINGS

Everything that can be invented has been invented.

-Charles H. Duell,
Commissioner of
U.S. Office of Patents, 1899

A woman is visiting her husband in the nursing home. All of the sudden he sneezes, covering his mouth at the same time.

"I'm proud of you," his wife says. "After all these years, you've finally learned to put your hand over your mouth."

The husband remarks, "Of course. How else was I going to catch my teeth?"

• • •

A guy comes home and finds his wife, a noted psychic, standing at the front door with a baseball bat in hand.

"You no good louse," she growled, "and just where were you until 3 a.m. tomorrow morning?"

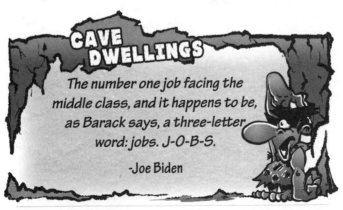

CAVE DWELLINGS

The number one job facing the middle class, and it happens to be, as Barack says, a three-letter word: jobs. J-O-B-S.

-Joe Biden

A dietician is conducting a seminar before a huge crowd. He tells the folks, "Much of the food we eat today is extremely unhealthful. Red meat is dangerous. Many vegetables are sprayed with pesticides and are unsafe. Drinking water can be contaminated. However, there is one food that is far and away the most dangerous of all. Can anyone tell me what it is?"

Following a long pause, a man in the back sticks his hand up and yells, "Wedding cake!"

• • •

A married couple are at a wishing well. The husband throws in a penny and makes a wish. The wife goes to do the same, but leans over too far and falls in. The husband looks deep down into the well and says, "Wow, it really works!"

• • •

"That young couple next door are so lovely," says Ethel to her husband. "In the morning, when he leaves the house, he kisses her goodbye, and every evening he comes home with flowers. Why can't you do something sweet like that?"

"Because I don't even know her."

A pair of elderly couples were chatting at dinner when one of the husbands said, "Bentley, how was that memory clinic you went to last week?"

"Great," answered Bentley. "We were taught all the latest and greatest memory helpers - association, visualization - that kind of stuff."

"Sounds good ... I might like to take a class. What was the name of it?"

Bentley's mind went blank. Then he suddenly smiled and said, "What do you call that flower that's red with a long stem and thorns?"

His buddy said, "You mean a rose?"

Bentley said, "Yeah, that's it," then turned to his wife and asked, "What was the name of that memory clinic, Rose?"

CAVE DWELLINGS

Every city I go to is an opportunity to paint, whether it's Omaha or Hawaii.

-Tony Bennett

As the casket is being carried out after a woman's funeral service, the pallbearers bump into a wall. The husband hears a faint moan, opens the casket and finds out that his wife is still alive!

Ten years later, the woman dies "again" and another funeral is held. At the end of the service, as the casket is being carried toward the door, the husband shouts, "Watch out for the wall!"

• • •

A couple gets married and has a baby. But the marriage is a rocky one, and two years into it, they separate. However, as they say, love conquers all and they decide to live together again. Everything is going swimmingly so the woman asks the fellow to marry her again.

"That's crazy!" exclaims the guy. "You expect me to marry a woman with a kid?!"

• • •

Wife: Honey, I've got some good news and bad news about the car.

Hubby: Gimme the good news first.

Wife: The air bag works.

The couple's married life was extremely difficult with Aunt Ethel living under the same roof for fourteen long years. Finally, the demanding and overbearing old woman died.

After the funeral was over, the wife confessed to her husband, "Honey, if I didn't love you as I do, I don't think I would have been able to put up with your Aunt Ethel for all these years."

Her stunned husband said, "My Aunt Ethel? I thought she was your Aunt Ethel!!"

• • •

A woman is standing before the judge in a packed courtroom. The judge asks, "What is it that you stole from the grocery store, ma'am?"

"Only a small can of a half dozen peaches," pleaded the woman.

"That'll be six nights in jail- one night for each stolen peach," declares the judge.

The woman is crestfallen. She looks like she's just about to faint when her husband shouts out from the back of the courtroom, "She stole a can of peas too!"

A married couple were in a horrible accident where the wife's face was severely burned. The doctor told her that they couldn't graft skin from her body because she was too thin. The husband offered to donate some of his own skin and the doctor advised that it would have to come from his buttocks.

Arrangements were made for the operation, the surgery took place and the result was a resounding success. The wife looked as radiant as ever, her face revealing not one iota of the ordeal she'd experienced.

She was overcome with emotion and said to her husband, "Dear, I can't possibly thank you enough for the sacrifice you made."

"Honey," he answered, "I get all the thanks I need every time I see your mother kiss you on the cheek."

CAVE DWELLINGS

Anne was a great girl. Hopefully she would have been a Belieber.

-Justin Bieber, during his visit to the Anne Frank House

Wally took his mother-in-law by complete surprise when he presented her with a delicately scented, beautifully wrapped birthday gift. She unwrapped the present and opened the box to find a beautiful pair of earrings and a loaded handgun.

"Why, Wally, these are really gorgeous, but why the gun?"

"That's to pierce your ears with."

• • •

Q: What do you have when your mother-in-law drives off a cliff in your brand new Mercedes?

A: Mixed emotions.

Q: What's the penalty for bigamy?

A: Two mothers-in-law.

• • •

One cannibal says to the other, "You know, I really don't care for my mother-in-law."

The other cannibal replies, "Just eat your vegetables then."

GOLF JOKES

A husband and wife, both golf fanatics, were discussing the future as they sat by a warm fireplace. "Dear," the wife said, "if I died, would you remarry?"

The husband responded, "Well, if something were to happen to you in the near future, I guess so. After all, we're not exactly senior citizens."

"Would you live in this house with her?" the wife asked.

"I would think so."

She continued, "How about my car? Would she get that?"

"I don't see why not."

"What about my golf clubs? Would you give them to her too?"

"Oh, goodness gracious no, never," the husband exclaimed. "She's left-handed."

A guy had been stranded on an island for ages. One day as he was walking on the beach, a beautiful woman in a wet suit emerged from the surf. "Hey, cutie pie. Have you been here long?" she asked.

"I reckon about ten years."

"Do you smoke?"

"Oh, what I'd do for a cigarette!" he moaned.

With that, she unzipped a pocket in the sleeve of her wet suit, pulled out a pack of cigarettes, lit one and gave it to him.

"I guess it's been a long while since you've had a drink, huh?"

"You got that right," he said.

She pulled out a flask from another pocket, gave it to him and he took a long, hard swig.

"I bet you haven't played around in a while either," she cooed as she began to unzip the front of her wet suit.

Positively wide-eyed with anticipation, he gasped, "Don't tell me you have a set of golf clubs in there too!?!"

At a hoity-toity country club which strictly enforced the rules of golf, a member saw that a guest of the club had his ball five inches in front of the tee markers.

The member hurriedly went over to the guest and said, "Sir, I don't know whether you've ever played here before, but we have very stringent rules about placing your tee at or behind the markers before driving the ball."

The guest looked the snooty club member right in the eye and retorted, "First, I've never played here before. Second, I don't care about your rules. And third, this is my second shot."

CAVE DWELLINGS

It's not the most intellectual job in the world, but I do have to know the letters.

-Vanna White,
Wheel of Fortune game show hostess

A REALLY DUMB HILLBILLY JOKE

A family of three from bucolic parts unknown was touring New York City. They walked into the Empire State Building together and the mother paused to view the magnificent art in the lobby.

The father and son went on ahead and, for the first time in their lives, saw an elevator. They were perplexed by the sideways sliding doors and couldn't imagine what the little room was for.

Just then, an elderly woman walked up and hit the button. The doors opened and she stepped in. The boy and his dad watched as the doors closed and the little round numbers went higher and higher. Then they paused and dropped back down. A little bell sounded, the doors opened and out stepped a voluptuous, eighteen-year-old beauty that any country boy would be proud to have as a kissin' cousin.

The father was simply amazed and, keeping his eye on the elevator, tapped the boy on the shoulder. "Billy-Bob," he said intently, "go get your mother."

"THERE'S A FLY IN MY SOUP" AND OTHER WAITER JOKES

An old fellow orders a bowl of soup at a restaurant. The waiter brings him the soup and starts to walk away. The old guy beckons to the waiter and says, "Taste this soup."

"Is it too hot?" the waiter asks.

The old man shakes his head. "Taste it."

The waiter asks, "Is it too cold?"

"Taste it," the senior responds.

"Is it too spicy?" the waiter asks.

"I said, taste the soup."

Now the waiter is totally exasperated. "Okay, okay, I'll taste it ... Where's the spoon?"

"Ah-ha!" says the old man gleefully.

A waiter dies suddenly and his widow is so distraught she seeks out a medium, who assures her that she can speak to her husband.

At the appointed time, the widow goes to a séance, presses her hands on the table and calls out, "Seymour, Seymour, speak to me!"

There's a terrible shriek and some scary noises followed by a faint voice which cries out, "Sorry, it's not my table!"

• • •

A man and a woman were at a fancy restaurant. They had placed their orders, but as the waitress was returning to bring their drinks, she noticed the man's head disappear under the tablecloth.

"Pardon me, ma'am, but I think your husband just slid under the table."

The woman calmly looked up at her and replied firmly, "No, my date just slid under the table. My husband just walked in the door."

"Waiter, there's a fly in my soup!"

"Please be quiet, Sir, everyone will want one!"

• • •

"Waiter, there's a fly in my soup!"

"I'm sorry, Sir, that's chicken noodle. You should have gotten the cockroach with that."

• • •

"Waiter, there's a fly in my soup!"

"Oh, Heavens no, Sir. He's not in your soup. He's been stuck to that bowl for weeks!"

• • •

If you ordered pasta and antipasta, would you still have an appetite?

CAVE DWELLINGS

I'd be willing to bet you, if I was a betting man, that I have never bet on baseball.

-Pete Rose

DUMB THINGS TO THINK ABOUT

• Is a vegetarian allowed to eat animal crackers?

• What do you say when an atheist sneezes?

• What if the Hokey Pokey is what it's all about?

• How would you do the YMCA in Chinese?

• When cheese gets its picture taken, what does it say?

• If you are cross-eyed and dyslexic at the same time, would you see okay?

• Why do you press harder on a remote control when you know the battery is dead?

• What is a picture of a thousand words worth?

• How do you draw a blank?

• Is there a time limit on fortune cookie predictions?

• Since bread is square, why is sandwich meat round?

• Would the ocean be deeper without sponges?

• How come you never see the headline "Psychic Wins Lottery"?

• Why is a carrot more orange than an orange?

• If you locked a humidifier and a de-humidifier in a room, who would win?

• What happened to Preparations A through G?

• What was the best thing before sliced bread?

• Is half of a large intestine a semi-colon?

• If you were given an order to disobey all orders would you disobey that order?

• Does Italy's Tower of Pisa look straight to a leaning tourist?

BAR JOKES

Steinmetz was sentenced to 20 years of solitary confinement. Bored to death after about two years of his jail stay, he spotted an ant crawling across the floor of his cell. This inspired him to think, "I've got plenty of time to kill ... I'll train this ant to do tricks."

Train him he did, first to do really simple things, then to do flips and somersaults. Steinmetz eventually taught the ant to juggle, to sing and even to do impressions of George Clooney, Bill Clinton, and Donald Trump.

When Steinmetz's sentence was finally over, he left the prison with the ant and the knowledge that he had a surefire show biz act. But before seeking out an agent, the man decided to celebrate his freedom with a drink. He went into a tavern, sat down and placed the ant on the bar in front of him.

As the bartender approached, Steinmetz said, "See this ant?"

"Sure do," the bartender exclaimed as he squashed the ant under his thumb. "Now what's your pleasure?"

A hotel desk clerk gets a call at four in the morning. "Shay, can you tell me what time the bar opens?" asks a rather sloshed fellow.

"11 A.M."

A bit later, the clerk gets another call from the same guy, who's now even more plastered. He slurs, "What time doesh the bar open?"

"Same time as I told you before, sir- 11 A.M."

An hour passes by and the clerk receives one more call from the drunk, who is definitely three sheets to the wind. "Shay, what timejushay shat shuy bar openshup?"

"11 A.M., sir. But if you want, you can order in and we'll send up room service."

"Lissten Buddy, I don' wanna ged in, I wanna ged out."

• • •

A bartender walked over to a guy with a frog on his head and said, "Hey, where'd you get that?"

"Believe it or not," the frog croaked, "it started out as a wart on my butt."

A guy sporting a snootful leaves a bar, waves down a taxi and says to the cabbie, "Take me to the corner of 45th and 5th."

"This is the corner of 45th and 5th," responds the cabbie.

"Thanks," the drunk belched, "but next time don't drive so fast."

• • •

A brain walks into a bar and the bartender says, "Sorry, I can't serve you."

"Why not?" asks the brain.

"You're already out of your head."

CAVE DWELLINGS

I believe that people would be alive today if there were a death penalty.

-Nancy Reagan

Two guys are sitting at a bar and become quite tipsy. The first guy says, "Say, where are you from?"

The second fellow says, "I'm from Miami."

The first guy replies, "Really? I'm from Miami, too. What high school did you go to?"

The second guy answers, "St. Joe's."

"Incredible!" remarks the first guy. "Me, too!"

"Wow!" says the second guy. "What year did you graduate?"

"'83."

"My gosh. I graduated in '83, too!"

"Looks like we're in for a long one tonight," the bartender sighs to one of the other customers. "The O'Malley twins are drunk again."

• • •

A bartender says to the customer, "What'll it be?"

"I'll have a martinus."

"You mean a martini, right?"

"If I wanted two of 'em, I'd order two of 'em."

A guy stepped up to the bar and ordered a martini. Before drinking it, he delicately removed the olive from the glass and put it into a small jar he took from his pocket.

After downing the drink, he ordered another and again took the olive from it and placed it into the jar. He repeated this process several times until the jar was full of olives. He then paid the bar tab and staggered out.

A customer who saw what had gone on said to the bartender, "Boy, that was really weird."

The bartender answered, "What's so odd about that? His wife sent him out for a jar of olives."

CAVE DWELLINGS

I'll fight Lloyd Honeyghan for nothing, if the price is right.

-Marlon Starling,
boxer

A guy walks into a bar with a cat perched on his head. The bartender gives him a beer and says, "Look. I don't know if you're aware of it, but there's a cat sitting on your head."

The guy says, "So what? I always wear a cat on my head on Friday."

"But today is Saturday," says the bartender.

"Oh, gosh," says the fellow. "I must look like a real idiot."

• • •

A pregnant woman walks into a bar, and is soon approached by a guy who says, "Can I sit here with you?"

She says, "No, I'm expecting someone."

CAVE DWELLINGS

What's Walmart?
Do they like make walls there?

-Paris Hilton

A middle-aged fellow stops into a bar for a nightcap. He strikes up a conversation with the bartender and says, "I just went to my first night school class."

"Really... what'd you learn?" asks the bartender.

"I learned to write."

"Hey, on your first day? That's terrific! What did you write?"

"Dunno...I can't read."

• • •

A guy walks into a bar and orders two martinis. The bartender serves them and says, "If it's all the same to you, pal, I could have made a double and used one glass."

The guy says, "Oh, I know, but my best buddy died and, just before he did, I promised him I'd order him a drink every time I came in here."

The next week the guy comes back and says to the bartender, "I'll have a martini."

The bartender says, "And one for your buddy, too?"

He says, "Oh, no. This is for my buddy. I'm on the wagon."

A pirate walks into a bar with a paper towel on his head. The bartender says, "What's up with the paper towel?"

The pirate says, "Arrrrr...there's a bounty on me head!"

• • •

A duck waddles into a bar. The bartender says, "Hey, pal, your pants are down around your ankles!"

• • •

A number sixteen walks into a bar and orders a beer. The bartender says, "Sorry, I can't serve you."

"Why not?"

"Because you're under twenty-one."

CAVE DWELLINGS

Solutions are not the answer.

-President Richard Nixon

An inkjet cartridge walks into a bar. The bartender asks, "Are you looking for a refill?"

• • •

A five-dollar bill walks into a saloon. The bartender says, "You'll have to leave. This is a singles' bar."

• • •

A fish goes into a bar. The bartender says, "What can I get you?"

The fish says, "Water."

• • •

A bear walks into a bar and asks the bartender for a gin ....and tonic.

The bartender says, "Sure, but why the big pause?"

The bear replies, "I was born with 'em!"

CAVE DWELLINGS

Rarely is the question asked,
"Is our children learning?"

-President George W. Bush

DUMB GENIE JOKES

An elderly woman was rocking on her front porch when her dog, Rover, appeared with a lamp in his mouth. The woman took the lamp from the dog and- poof! – the proverbial Genie appeared. The Genie said, "Your three wishes will be my commands."

The old lady said, "Well, for one, I'd like to be rich."

The Genie clapped her hands, turning the old lady's rocking chair into solid gold and said, "Your next wish?"

"I would like to be young and beautiful again."

The Genie clapped her hands again and her wish was granted. The woman was once again young and beautiful. "And your final wish?" asked the Genie.

"Well, I haven't enjoyed the company of a good-looking beau in quite some time. Could you possibly make Rover my handsome prince?"

The Genie once again clapped her hands and then disappeared as the dog became a gorgeous hunk. His resemblance to Brad Pitt made the woman shiver with excitement. He nuzzled up to the rejuvenated young maiden and whispered in her ear, "Now aren't you sorry you had me neutered?"

• • •

Murphy finds an old lamp and rubs it. Poof! A Genie appears and says, "You have three wishes."

"Oh, boy," says Murphy, "I love my Guinness, so how about a bottle of Guinness that'll never be empty?"

Poof! His wish is granted. Murphy takes a swig of the neverending bottle, thinks for a second, and then asks, "I get three wishes, Genie, right?"

"Absolutely," responds the genie.

"Great. I'll take two more of these!"

CAVE DWELLINGS

Of all the things I've lost, it's my mind I miss the most.

-Ozzy Osbourne

HUNTING AND FISHING HILARITY

Two guys are out hunting when they come across some tracks in the woods. The first guy says, "Look, moose tracks."

The second one says, "No. Those are deer tracks. I know deer tracks when I see 'em."

A few moments later, they both get run over by a train.

• • •

Two fellows are hunting in the woods when one of them keels over and falls to the ground. The second guy panics. He calls 911 from his cell phone and says, "Help, help! I'm out here hunting with my friend and he suddenly dropped to the ground. I think he's dead."

The 911 operator responds, "Now, now. Calm down. First thing, you have to make sure he's dead."

BANG, BANG!

The hunter says, "Okay, he's dead. Now what do we do?"

Then there was the fellow who went to buy some camouflage clothes, but he couldn't find any.

. . .

A novice hunter came back to the lodge and proudly said, "I shot an elk!"

"How do you know it was an elk?" asked one of the members.

"By his membership card."

. . .

Pete takes the grieving widow of his old fishing buddy out in his bass boat to show her just where the fatal accident occurred the day before. After circling the spot for twenty minutes he looks up and says, "I know this is around the place where Al stood up and fell in. I'm sure this is where I radioed the ranger and he brought the police, but for the life of me, I can't find it."

"Find what?" sniffles Al's widow.

Pete answers, "The chalk outline."

There was a sign on a bait and tackle shop which read, "Fishing Tickle." A customer walked in, told the owner of the spelling error and then asked, "How long has that sign been like that?"

"Oh, for many years," replied the owner.

"Hasn't anyone else told you of the error?" questioned the man.

"Oh, sure. That's how I get customers."

• • •

A hunter goes into a butcher's store and asks for a duck. The butcher says, "We're all out of duck. I've got plenty of chicken, though. How about a chicken?"

"Oh, that's just fine," complains the hunter. "How am I gonna tell my wife that I shot a chicken?"

CAVE DWELLINGS

I want Brooklyn to be christened, but don't know into what religion yet.

-David Beckham, on his newborn son

And then there were the two hunters who were driving through the woods and came upon a fork in the road where a sign read "BEAR LEFT"- so they went home.

• • •

Three old geezers were sitting on a bench in New York City's Central Park. The one in the middle was reading a newspaper while the other two were pretending to fish. A policeman on the beat watched them as they baited imaginary hooks, cast their lines and reeled in their fake catches.

"Do you know these two?" the cop asked the guy reading the paper.

"Sure. They're buddies of mine."

"Well, they're disturbin' the other people. You better get them outta here!"

"Yes, officer," said the guy. With that, he furiously began rowing.

• • •

Upon inspecting the hunter's credentials, the game warden said, "This is last year's license."

"I know," said the hunter. "I'm only shooting at the deer I missed last year."

Q: What kind of ammo do sick hunters fire?

A: Flu shots.

Q: What did the lion say when he saw two hunters in a jeep?

A: Meals on wheels!

• • •

A fishing boat goes down with only one man surviving and he's washed ashore on a remote island inhabited by cannibals. They capture him and tie him to a stake, where they proceed to nick him with their spears and drink his blood.

This goes on for two weeks. The guy can't take it any longer and asks to see the chief. When the cannibal leader arrives the guy says, "Look, chief...either let me go or kill me. I'm tired of being stuck for the drinks."

• • •

At Sunday school, the teacher was leading a class discussion on what Noah might have done to pass time on the Ark.

"I think he went fishing," said one little girl.

The little boy sitting beside her gave her a look and piped up, "What...with only two worms?!"

A fisherman was arrested and brought to court for having caught fourteen more striped bass than the law allowed.

The judge asked, "How do you plead?"

"Guilty, your Honor," was the reply.

"That'll be 75 dollars plus costs," said the judge.

The fisherman paid the fine, then inquired of the judge, "Your Honor, if you don't mind, would it be possible to make some copies of the court record to take home to show my buddies?"

• • •

An avid angler on a fishing trip was at it for almost two weeks before he caught his first fish. When he got back to his hotel, he texted his wife: "I've got one. She's a real beauty...weighs seven pounds. I'll be home in a couple of days."

His wife responded with this text: "I've got one as well. She also weighs seven pounds and is a real beauty, too. Come home at once."

• • •

Q: Why couldn't Batman go fishing?

A: Because Robin ate all the worms.

A guy goes ice fishing in Minnesota for the first time. He's not having any luck at all, but another guy sitting close by is pulling up fish left and right. The novice ice fisherman asks the guy, "What's the trick?"

The ice fisherman mumbles, "Mmumottameepdammrmsmmrm."

"What'd you say?"

"Mmumottameepdammrmsmmrm."

"I still don't understand you."

With that, the ice fisherman opens his thermos, spits into it a couple of times and then says, "I said you've got to keep the worms warm."

CAVE DWELLINGS

Smoking kills. If you're killed, you've lost a very important part of your life.

-Brooke Shields

A guy saw a fisherman catch a giant trout, only to throw it back into the water. A few minutes later, he nabbed another huge trout but tossed that away, too. Then he caught a little trout, smiled and put it into his cooler for safekeeping. The guy who was watching the fisherman asked, "How come you threw away the big fish and kept the small one?"

The fisherman replied, "Small frying pan."

• • •

A couple of Eskimos went fishing on an extremely frigid day. They lit a fire in the bottom of their kayak to warm up, but moments later the blaze raged out of control and their boat sank.

The moral of the story: You can't have your kayak and heat it, too.

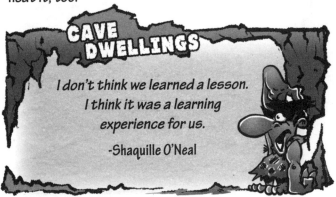

CAVE DWELLINGS

I don't think we learned a lesson. I think it was a learning experience for us.

-Shaquille O'Neal

A guy is eating a bald eagle and gets caught by the game warden. He's brought to trial for killing an endangered species. The judge says, "Are you aware that eating a bald eagle is a federal offense?"

The guy answers, "Yes, but I have an explanation... I got lost in the woods and didn't have anything to eat for two weeks. I saw this bald eagle swooping down for fish in the lake. I figured I might be able to steal some fish as the eagle grabbed them. Unfortunately, when I went to grab for the fish, my fist hit the eagle in the head and killed 'im. I reckoned that, since the eagle was dead, I might as well eat it since it would be a waste to just let it rot."

After a brief recess, the judge comes back with his ruling. "Due to the extreme conditions you endured, added to the fact that the bald eagle's death was accidental rather than intentional, I find you not guilty."

As an aside, the judge asks the guy, "By the way, what does a bald eagle taste like?"

The guy responds, "Gee, Judge. I guess the best way to describe it is that it tastes like a cross between an owl and an egret."

LITTLE JOHNNY JOKES

A science teacher was giving a lesson on the circulation of blood and said, "Now, class, if I stood on my head the blood would rush into it and I would turn red in the face. But how come when I stand up straight the blood doesn't run into my feet?"

Little Johnny yelled from the back of the classroom, "Because your feet aren't empty."

• • •

The teacher was asking the class about what their parents do for a living. "What does your Daddy do?" Mrs. Jones asked Little Johnny.

Little Johnny replied, "My daddy's dead."

"Oh, I'm sorry," said Mrs. Jones. "But what did he do before he died?"

"He sort of grabbed his chest and fell over."

"Hey, Grandpa, can you make a noise like a frog?" asked Little Johnny.

"Why do you want me to do that, Johnny?"

"Because Mom said when you croak, we're goin' to Disney World!"

• • •

The class was assigned to write about something unusual that happened. When Little Johnny was called on, he got up and began to read, "Dad fell in the well last week..."

"My gosh!" interrupted his teacher. "Is he okay?"

"He must be," said Johnny. "He stopped calling for help yesterday."

CAVE DWELLINGS

It's not that I dislike many people. It's just that I don't like many people.

-Bryant Gumbel

Little Johnny went into a supermarket, picked out a big box of laundry detergent and went to the checkout. The grocer asked Johnny if he had a lot of laundry to do.

"Nah," said Johnny, "I'm gonna wash my dog."

"You shouldn't wash him with this," said the grocer. "It's real strong stuff and could make him sick or even worse."

But Johnny insisted on buying the suds. A few days later, he went back to the store to buy some candy. The grocer asked him how the dog was doing.

Johnny said, "Oh, he died."

The grocer said he was sorry to hear that but repeated that he was afraid the detergent would be extremely harmful to the dog.

Johnny said, "I don't think it was the detergent that did him in."

The grocer asked, "What was it then?"

"I think it was the spin cycle."

The teacher asks Little Johnny if he knows his numbers. He says, "Yes. My father taught me."

"Good. Then what comes after four?"

"Five," answers Johnny.

"What comes after eight?"

"Nine," says Johnny.

"Excellent," says the teacher. "Sounds like your dad taught you well. And what comes after ten?"

"A jack."

• • •

Little Johnny's mother, in an attempt to get him to stop sucking his thumb, told him that if he continued to do so his stomach would get bigger and bigger until it burst.

Later that day they went to the supermarket, where Johnny saw a very pregnant woman. Embarrassed that he was staring at her, the woman said, "You don't know me. You shouldn't be looking at me like that."

Johnny replied, "I may not know you, but I know what you've been doing."

A kindergarten teacher was reading the "Three Little Pigs" to her class. She came to the part of the story where the first pig was trying to gather the building materials for his home.

She read, "...And so the pig went up to the man with the wheelbarrow full of straw and said, 'Excuse me sir, but may I have some of that straw to build my house?'"

The teacher paused and then asked the class, "And what do you think that man said?"

Little Johnny raised his hand and said, "I know. He said, 'Holy crap! A talking pig!'"

• • •

"Do you know about the birds and the bees?" asks Little Johnny's father.

"I don't want to know!" Little Johnny says, bursting into tears.

Johnny's father is perplexed and asks him what's wrong. Little Johnny sobs, "First, there was no Santa Claus, then no Easter Bunny, and then no Tooth Fairy. If you're gonna tell me that grownups don't really have sex, I've got nothing left to believe in."

One Sunday morning in church, Little Johnny said, "Mommy, I gotta pee."

His mother said, "It's not polite to say the word 'pee' in church. From now on, if you have to pee, just say that you have to 'whisper.'"

The next week, Johnny was in church with his father when he said, "Daddy, I have to whisper."

His dad said, "Okay, just whisper in my ear."

• • •

Little Johnny asks his mother her age. She replies, "Gentlemen don't ask a lady how old she is."

Johnny then asks his mother how much she weighs. His mother once again answers, "Gentlemen don't ask ladies that question."

Johnny then asks, "Why did Daddy leave you?"

His mother says, "You shouldn't ask that."

A bit later, Johnny gets into some mischief. Rummaging through his mother's purse, he comes across her driver's license. He runs up to his mother and excitedly says, "I know all about you now. You're 35 years old, you weigh 125 pounds and Daddy left you because you got an 'F' in sex!"

Little Johnny was in his kindergarten class when the teacher asked the kids what their dads did for a living. The usual jobs came up- fireman, salesman, accountant, policeman- but Johnny was uncharacteristically shy about giving an answer.

Finally, the teacher said, "Johnny, how about you? What does your father do for a living?"

Johnny murmured, "My dad's a circus freak who bites the heads off small animals."

The startled teacher quickly ended that segment of class and sent the other kids off to do some coloring. Then, she took little Johnny aside and said, "Is that really true about your father?"

"No," said Johnny, "but I was afraid the other kids would make fun of me if I said that he's really a lawyer."

CAVE DWELLINGS

I don't diet. I just don't eat as much as I'd like to.

-Linda Evangelista, model

At the ripe old age of three, Little Johnny began playing Superman. Every day, his mommy would pin a bright red bath towel on his blue t-shirt and he'd become the superhero.

Well, when it came time to enroll for kindergarten, the teacher was interviewing the caped Little Johnny and his mother. When the teacher asked him his name, Johnny answered politely, "Superman."

The teacher smiled at Johnny and his mother and asked his name again. Again, Johnny said, "Superman."

Now, the teacher was a bit concerned, so she said, "I will have to have your real name for my records."

Johnny bent over and whispered in her ear, "Clark Kent."

CAVE DWELLINGS

The president has kept all of the promises he intended to keep.

-George Stephanopolous

Little Johnny was in his backyard filling in a hole when his neighbor asked, "What are you doing, Johnny?"

"My goldfish died and I've just buried him," answered Johnny.

The sympathetic neighbor said, "I'm sorry to hear that, Johnny...Say, that seems like an awfully big hole for a goldfish."

Little Johnny replied, "That's because he's inside your stupid cat."

• • •

The teacher calls on Little Johnny during a vocabulary lesson and says, "Johnny, can you use the letter 'I' in a sentence?"

Little Johnny starts off with, "I is," but is immediately interrupted by the teacher.

"No, that's wrong, Johnny. You never say 'I is.' It's always 'I am.'"

"Okay," Johnny says. "I am the letter that comes after H."

A woman answers the phone and the voice says, "This is the principal's office at grammar school. We're calling about your son, Johnny. He's been telling unbelievable lies."

"I'll say he has," the woman responds. "I don't have a son."

• • •

"How do you spell the word 'straight'?" asked Mrs. Jones, to her third grade class.

From the back of the room, Little Johnny yelled, "S-T-R-A-I-G-H-T."

"Excellent," remarked the teacher. "And what does that mean, Johnny?"

"Without ice."

CAVE DWELLINGS

Two things are infinite: the universe and human stupidity; and I'm not sure about the universe.

-Albert Einstein

Little Johnny is out fishing with his grandfather. They're sitting by the river, waiting and waiting for the fish to bite. Finally, to break up the boredom, little Johnny's grandfather decides to teach his grandson a lesson.

He takes out a flask of whiskey from his hip pocket and pours it into a glass. Then he reaches for the bait, pulls out a couple of worms and puts them in the glass full of liquor. The worms become lifeless almost immediately.

"Look here, Johnny," his grandfather says. "See that? Those worms have died. What does that tell you, son?"

"Simple, Grandpa," little Johnny answers. "Drink whiskey and you won't get worms."

CAVE DWELLINGS

We have a lot of kids who don't know what work means. They think work is a four-letter word.

-Hillary Clinton

SPORTS JOKES

The Seven Dwarfs were walking through the woods one day when they all fell into a deep, dark hole. Snow White, who was following along, peered over the edge and yelled down to the fallen dwarfs.

From the depths of the seemingly bottomless pit, a voice hollered back, "The Jaguars are going to win the Super Bowl!"

Snow White muttered to herself, "Thank God- at least Dopey is alive!"

• • •

Q: Why was the fighter nicknamed "Rembrandt"?

A: His face was always on the canvas.

• • •

Two visitors from Greece went to a baseball game. After a few innings, one turned to the other and asked, "Do you have any idea what this is all about?"

The other replied, "No, it's all English to me."

Four old duffers had a Saturday morning 8 o'clock tee time for years. On one such morning, they noticed a guy watching them as they teed off. At every tee, he caught up with them and had to wait.

When they reached the fifth tee, the guy walked up to the foursome and handed them a card which read, "I am deaf and mute. May I play through?"

The old duffers were outraged and signaled to him that nobody plays through their group. He'd just have to bide his time.

On the eighth hole, one of the foursome was on the fairway lining up his second shot. All of the sudden he got bopped in the back of the head by the stinging force of a golf ball. He turned around and looked back at the tee angrily.

There stood the deaf mute, frantically waving his arm in the air, holding up four fingers.

• • •

The punch drunk fighter was nearly killed in a horse riding mishap. He fell from the horse and was almost trampled to death. Fortunately, the Walmart manager came out and unplugged it.

Two runners were trailing the pack in the marathon. The guy who was second-to-last was poking fun at the runner behind him. "Hey, how does it feel to be last?"

"Well, if you must know," said the other guy... And then he dropped out.

• • •

An Oakland Raiders fan had two extra tickets to the game so he left them under his windshield wiper in the stadium parking lot. When he returned to his car after the game, there were four more tickets.

CAVE DWELLINGS

So, where's the Cannes Film Festival being held this year?

-Christina Aguilera

DUMB BLONDE JOKES

Q: How come blonde jokes are so short?

A: So brunettes can remember them.

• • •

The hysterical blonde charged into the police station screaming that her car had been stolen.

"Calm down, ma'am," advised the desk sergeant. "Do you have a description of the suspect?"

"No," the blonde replied, fighting back tears, "but I did manage to get the license plate number."

• • •

A ventriloquist is telling a dumb-blonde joke when an offended platinum-haired woman in the audience yells out, "You have no right to stereotype blondes that way!"

The ventriloquist becomes flustered and tries to apologize but she cuts him off, saying, "You stay out of this! I'm talking to that little twerp on your knee!"

A blonde arrived home to find her apartment had been broken into and ransacked. Almost hysterical at this violation of her home, she called the police and a K-9 unit nearby responded within the minute.

The officer knocked at her door with the police dog on its lead and showed his ID. At this, the woman became even more upset, breaking down and sobbing uncontrollably. When she finally calmed down, the officer asked her what was wrong.

The woman sniffed back her tears and wailed, "Being burglarized is bad enough. Now they send me a blind policeman!"

• • •

Gertrude's car was pelted in a driving hailstorm one night, resulting in hundreds of dents. The next day she visits a body shop to get it fixed. The repairman figures he'll have a little fun with her and tells Gertrude that all she has to do is blow into the exhaust pipe really hard and the dents will pop out.

Gertrude goes home and blows furiously into the tailpipe. When her blonde roommate asks what Gertrude's doing, she explains what the repairman advised her to do. "But it doesn't work," she says.

"Hellooo," says the blonde. "You gotta roll up the windows first."

Paris Hilton goes into a department store and tells the salesman she's looking for a blue curtain. He shows her a wide selection of blue fabrics and then asks, "What size curtains do you need?"

She answers aloofly, "Just 19 inches."

Surprised, he says, "19 inches! What room are they for?"

She replies snottily, "I only need one, and it's not for a room. It's for my computer monitor."

The intimidated salesman sputters, "But ma'am, computers do not have curtains."

To which Paris Hilton sneers to the lowly clerk, "HELLOOoooooo.... I've got Windows!"

CAVE DWELLINGS

*If being sane is being normal,
I'd rather be completely mental.*

-Angelina Jolie

STUPID ANIMAL JOKES

Three pigs are in the barnyard. The first one says, "Oink, oink."

The second pig says, "Oink, oink, oink."

The third pig says, "Moooo."

The other two pigs do a double take. Overhearing the third pig, the farmer asks, "What did you say?"

"Mooooooo."

"That's crazy," says the farmer. "Pigs don't say, 'moooo'!"

"I know," the third pig says. "But I'm trying to learn a second language."

• • •

Q: Why do elephants paint their toenails red?
A: So they can hide in cherry trees.

Q: How come you never see elephants hiding in trees?
A: Because they're really good at it.

Two turtles go fishing and pack a cooler with sandwiches and a six-pack. After five days of walking, they find a great spot at the lake, but they've forgotten the bottle opener. One turtle says to the other, "Why don't you go back and get the opener?"

The other turtle says, "No way. You'll eat all the food while I'm gone."

The first turtle says, "I promise I won't. Just hurry."

The second turtle leaves. Nine days later there's no sign of him. Finally, the first turtle opens up one of the sandwiches. The second turtle pops out from behind a rock and hollers, "I knew it! Now I'm not going!"

CAVE DWELLINGS

I won't go into a big spiel about reincarnation, but the first time I was in the Gucci store in Chicago was the closest I've ever felt to home.

-Kanye West

Q: What's the number one cause of death for hamsters?

A: Falling asleep at the wheel.

• • •

A snake has terribly poor eyesight. What little vision he has is failing fast so he goes to the optometrist. The eye doctor fits him with some glasses and, immediately, there's significant improvement.

A week goes by and the doctor checks on the snake to see how he's doing with his new spectacles. The snake says, "They're great, Doc, but now I'm being treated for depression."

"Why depression?" asks the doctor.

"Until I got my eyeglasses, I didn't realize I'd been dating a garden hose."

CAVE DWELLINGS

*Always be sincere,
even if you don't mean it.*

-President Harry S Truman

A rabbit hopped into a butcher shop and asked, "Do you have any carrots?"

"No," said the butcher.

The next day the rabbit showed up and said, "Have any carrots?"

"If I told you once, I told you twice- The answer is NO," said the butcher.

The following day the rabbit appeared again and said, "Got any carrots?"

The butcher angrily replied, "N-O, NO! And if you come back in here again and ask for carrots, I'll hammer you to the wall by your ears!"

The next day the rabbit came back and asked, "Do you have any nails?"

"No," said the butcher.

"Good ... Do you have any carrots?"

• • •

Two caterpillars are strolling along in the park when one sees a butterfly go by, points up at it and says to the other, "You'll never get me up in one of those things."

AT THE PEARLY GATES

A crowd of husbands are about to enter through the Pearly Gates when St. Peter roars, "Hold it right there! I want all of you who were henpecked husbands while on Earth to form a line to my right. The rest of you stand to my left."

All but one husband stands on the henpecked line. St. Peter turns to the guy standing alone and says, "How about you? What's your story?"

He replies sheepishly, "My wife told me to stand here."

• • •

Every day this guy prays to God to let him win the lottery. He keeps promising to do all sorts of good deeds if God will only let him win the jackpot. Week after week he prays but never wins. Finally, one day he's talking to God and says, "I'm a good man. I've been praying faithfully. Can't you allow me to win the lottery?"

A booming voice from the heavens answers, "You gotta buy a ticket!"

There's a knock on the door of the Pearly Gates. St. Peter answers it and sees a guy there. St. Peter turns around to lead him in to his eternal bliss but the fellow disappears.

After a few moments, there's another knock. St. Peter answers it. It's the same guy. And as soon as St. Peter sees him, he vanishes again.

A bit later, there's another knock. St. Peter answers it one more time, sees the same guy, and says, "What is this, some kind of game you're playing?"

The guy answers, "No, they're trying to resuscitate me."

• • •

Q Who's the patron saint of e-mail?

A: St. Francis of a CC

CAVE DWELLINGS

You know the one thing that's wrong with this country? Everyone gets a chance to have their fair say.

-President Bill Clinton

DUMB Q&As

Why do mermaids wear seashells?
Because B-shells are too small and D-shells are
too big.

What do French people yell on the roller coaster?
"Yes!"

What do you get if you mix a car, a fly, and a dog?
A flying carpet

What does Miley Cyrus eat on Thanksgiving?
Twerkey

What do a Slinky and your boss have in common?
They're both fun to watch tumble down the stairs.

What do you do when you see a spaceman?
Park your car, man.

What was Beethoven's favorite fruit?
Ba-na-na-naaaaaa!

What was Adam and Eve's biggest problem?
They could never agree on who wore the plants in the
family.

How many drummers does it take to change a light bulb?
One- Two, and a-one, two, three, four...

How many stockbrokers does it take to change a light bulb?
Two- one to take the bulb out and drop it, and the other to try and sell it before it crashes.

How many car salesmen does it take to change a light bulb?
I have to work this out on my calculator but I think you will be pleasantly surprised.

How many divorced men does it take to change a light bulb?
It doesn't matter. They never get the house anyway.

How many South Americans does it take to change a light bulb?
A Brazilian!

What do you call a dog that hears voices?
A Shih-Tzu-Phrenic

Q: What do you do with a broken dog?
A: Get him fixed.

DUMB MEN JOKES

Q: What has eight arms and an IQ of 160?
A: Four men watching a football game.

Q: What makes a man think about a dinner by candlelight?
A: A power failure.

Q: What do you call a man with an opinion?
A: Wrong.

Q: Why do so few men end up in Heaven?
A: They never stop to ask directions.

Q: Why are most dumb blonde jokes one-liners?
A: So men can understand them.

Q: Why don't men have a mid-life crisis?
A: They're stuck in adolescence.

Q: What do men and mascara have in common?
A: They both run at the first sign of emotion.

Q: What's the difference between men and government bonds?
A: Bonds mature.

PRETTY DUMB, BUT PRETTY GOOD LAST LAUGHS

A guy was shopping for dinner at a supermarket when a beautiful redhead smiled and waved at him. He couldn't figure out where he knew her from but, nonetheless, he was thrilled at the attention until she walked up and said, "I think you're the father of one of my kids."

Taken aback, he initially denied it but then searched his memory. "Wait," he blurted out. "That night my buddies got me drunk and took all my clothes and set me out on Main Street and I wandered around until I came into this little bar and fell in the mud-wrestling pit and vomited all over the floor... Were you the stripper who took me home with her that night?"

"No," she answered coolly. "I'm your son's math teacher."

• • •

A Spanish magician announced to his audience, "I will disappear on the count of 3... Uno, dos..." and then –poof– he disappeared without a tres!

On a royal visit to London, President Obama was taking a horse-drawn carriage ride with the Queen of England. When one of the horses became overcome with foul-smelling flatulence, the Queen felt compelled to apologize. "I'm sorry, Mr. President, but I hope you understand that there are some things that even a Queen cannot control."

The president nodded and said, "I understand, but to tell you the truth, until you mentioned it, I thought it was one of the horses."

• • •

A New Yorker calls his mother who lives in Miami. She answers the phone with a very weak-sounding voice.

"Mom, you don't sound good. What's wrong?"

Very feebly she answers, "I haven't eaten in quite some time."

"How long has it been, Mom?"

"My last meal was 26 days ago."

"26 days! How come?"

"I didn't want to be caught with food in my mouth when you called."